FAVOURITE RECIPES
from the
KITCHEN GARDEN

*including a selection
of vegetarian dishes*

*with illustrations by
Helen Allingham RWS*

SALMON

Index

Cover pictures *front:* Cutting cabbages
back: A farm garden, Wiltshire *title page*: Shelling Peas By Birket Foster

Printed and Published by J. Salmon Ltd., Sevenoaks, England © Copyright

Leek Pasty

A flat, puff pastry pie filled with creamy leeks and sausages.

3 oz butter	3 eggs
1½ lbs leeks, trimmed and thinly sliced	¼ pint double cream
8 chipolata sausages	Salt and black pepper
Lard or oil for frying	¾ lb puff pastry

1 egg yolk beaten to glaze

Set oven to 425°F or Mark 7. Melt the butter in a large pan, stir in the leeks, cover and cook, stirring occasionally, until they are reduced almost to a purée. Uncover and cook for a few minutes longer to evaporate excess moisture. Meanwhile prick the sausages and fry until well browned all over. Beat together the eggs and cream and season well. Remove the pan of leeks from the heat and stir in the egg/cream mixture until it thickens slightly. Check the seasoning and set aside to cool until lukewarm. Halve the pastry and roll out on a floured surface to two 10 inch circles. Lay one circle on a lightly greased baking sheet and pile on the leek mixture. Arrange the sausages in a star pattern, dampen the pastry border and cover with the other circle and then seal the edge. Cut slits and brush with egg yolk. Bake for 10 minutes then reduce oven to 350°F or Mark 4 and bake for a further 30 to 35 minutes until the pastry is puffed and golden brown. Serve hot. Serves 6.

Marrow Pie

This is a variation of a form of pumpkin pie and is a useful way of using up a glut of vegetable marrows from the garden.

8 oz shortcrust pastry **Rind of ½ lemon and 1 teaspoon of juice**
2 oz jam - apricot is ideal **1½ tablespoons soft brown sugar**
1 egg, beaten **Pinch of ground nutmeg**
1 lb vegetable marrow, peeled, de-seeded and cut into small cubes

Set oven to 400°F or Mark 6. Roll out the pastry and line a lightly greased 8 inch flan dish. Spread the jam evenly over the pastry base. Boil the marrow until soft, then drain very well and leave to cool. Then stir in the egg, lemon rind and juice, sugar and nutmeg and beat until smooth. Turn into the pastry case and sprinkle a little more brown sugar and nutmeg over the top. Roll out the pastry trimmings, cut into strips and decorate the pie with a lattice pattern. Bake for 15 minutes, then reduce the oven temperature to 350°F or Mark 4 and bake for a further 15 minutes until the pastry is golden. Serve hot or cold with custard or cream. Serves 4 to 6. If desired 2 oz of currants or sultanas can be added to the mixture.

A cottage at Newchurch, Isle of Wight

French Beans in Mushroom Cream

A more luxurious way of serving French beans than normal.

1 lb young french beans	¹/₄ lb button mushrooms, halved or quartered
2 oz butter	Lemon juice
1 small onion, finely chopped	6 tablespoons single cream
	Salt and black pepper

Top and tail the beans. Drop into a large pan of fast boiling, salted water and cook briskly for about 10 minutes until tender but still crisp. Meanwhile, melt the butter in a large pan and fry the onion gently until soft and golden. Add the mushrooms, squeeze over a little lemon juice and cook gently for a further 3 to 5 minutes until softened slightly and golden. Drain the beans thoroughly and mix with the onion and mushrooms. Add the cream and season to taste. Return to a low heat, stirring gently and bring to simmering point. Simmer, bubbling, for 3 minutes to thicken the sauce then serve immediately. Serves 4.

Turnips and Gammon

A simple dish to prepare, yet one which makes a tasty meal.

1½ lb turnips, peeled and
    cut into ½ inch cubes
½ oz butter
¾ - 1 lb slice of gammon
    cut into ½ inch cubes

Black pepper
2 tablespoons chopped parsley
2 - 3 tablespoons single cream
Mushrooms and small tomatoes,
    grilled or baked, for garnish.

Boil the cubed turnips in salted water until just cooked, then drain. Meanwhile, melt the butter in a pan and fry the gammon slowly until cooked. Then add the turnip, season, toss carefully and cook for a further 5 minutes. Stir in the parsley and the cream, reheat and transfer to a warmed serving dish. Surround with the previously grilled or baked mushrooms and tomatoes and serve. Serves 4.

Stuffed Onions

This method of cooking stuffed onions keeps them whole and not overcooked on the outside.

4 large onions e.g. Spanish type	½ lb pork sausagemeat
1 oz butter	2 tablespoons fresh breadcrumbs
¼ teaspoon dried mixed herbs	1 tablespoon Worcestershire sauce
Salt and black pepper	Small whole tomatoes, baked, for garnish

Set oven to 400ºF or Mark 6. Wash the onion skins and trim off just sufficient root end to allow to stand upright. Stand in a pan of cold water, bring to the boil and simmer for 15 minutes. Drain and rinse in cold water to cool. Cut a slice off the top of each onion and discard the skin from the tops. Carefully remove most of the insides from the onions, leaving only about a two layer thickness. Chop the removed onion with the lids. Melt the butter in a frying pan, add the chopped onion and cook for a few minutes. Add the herbs, seasoning and sausagemeat, break up and mix well together and fry until the meat is lightly browned. Stir in the breadcrumbs and Worcestershire sauce. Use the mixture to fill each onion, stand them in a greased baking dish and put any spare filling in the dish. Arrange the small tomatoes around the onions and bake for 20 minutes. The onion skins are easily removed at table. Serves 4.

Buttered Broad Beans

In this recipe the broad beans are cooked in the pod, so they must be picked very young, no more than 4 to 5 inches long.

1 lb baby broad beans in their pods
2 oz butter, softened
1 tablespoon fresh chopped chervil
   or 2 teaspoons dried chervil

1 tablespoon finely chopped parsley
Lemon juice
Coarse salt and black pepper
Herb butter for topping

Top and tail the beans and cut each diagonally into 3 or 4 pieces. Drop into a bowl of cold water and leave until needed. Bring a pan of salted water to the boil, drain the beans and drop them in. Bring back to the boil and boil briskly for about 10 minutes or until tender. Meanwhile cream the butter with the herbs and a few drops of lemon juice. Drain the beans thoroughly, return to the pan and toss over a high heat for a minute or two, to dry off the excess moisture. Season to taste with freshly ground salt and pepper and serve very hot, topping each portion with a pat of herb butter. Serves 4.

Fried Parsnips and Potatoes with Eggs

A quick and economical light supper dish made from simple ingredients.

1 lb parsnips, scraped	1 oz butter
1 lb potatoes, peeled	4 eggs
6 rashers bacon, de-rinded and chopped	Salt and black pepper

Cut the parsnips and potatoes into slices of equal thickness and boil in separate pans of salted water for 6 to 8 minutes or until barely tender. Drain in a colander and leave to cool. Meanwhile, fry the chopped bacon in a large lidded frying pan until the fat is transparent. Add the parsnip and potato slices and fry, turning from time to time until golden brown. Remove from the heat. Spread the cooked slices of parsnips and potatoes and the bacon evenly over the bottom of the pan, form four hollows in them and carefully break an egg into each one. Season. Cover the pan and continue cooking until the eggs are set according to personal taste. Serve straight from the pan. Serves 4.

Quick Cauliflower Cheese

A simpler and different version of the standard English supper standby.

1 medium cauliflower head   **2 tablespoons Parmesan cheese, grated**
8 tablespoons Gruyère cheese, grated   **2 tablespoons fine, dry breadcrumbs**
4 tablespoons melted butter

Set oven to 400ºF or Mark 6. Prepare the cauliflower by breaking up into florets and preferably steam, or boil, until tender. Drain and put into a buttered baking dish. In a bowl, toss the cheeses with the breadcrumbs to combine and then incorporate the melted butter. Sprinkle this mixture over the cauliflower and bake for 10 to 15 minutes or until the cheese has melted and the topping is sizzling and golden. Serves 4.

Hot Red Cabbage

This vegetable is delicious served hot with roasts and casseroles.

2 oz butter	1½ lbs red cabbage, finely shredded
2 large cooking apples, peeled, cored and sliced	¼ pint cider vinegar
	4 oz redcurrant jelly

Melt the butter in a very large pan and add the apples and cabbage. Cover and sauté for 10 minutes, stirring occasionally. Add the vinegar, cover and cook very gently for 45 minutes to one hour, until the cabbage is just soft, stirring occasionally. Add the redcurrant jelly and mix in thoroughly. Cook for a further 15 minutes. Transfer to a warmed serving dish. Serves 4 to 6.

Sweet Corn Fritters

Served with maple syrup, these corn fritters make a delicious snack.

³/₄ lb cooked corn kernels, fresh or tinned
5 tablespoons double cream
4 tablespoons fine cornmeal (polenta)
2 teaspoons sugar

¹/₂ teaspoon baking powder
Pinch of salt
2 eggs, separated
Butter for frying

If using corn cobs, first boil until the kernels are tender then remove them with a sharp knife. Drain the corn kernels thoroughly. Purée all the ingredients, except the egg whites and the butter, in a food processor or blender. Whisk the egg whites in a bowl until stiff but not dry, then fold gently but thoroughly into the corn batter. Heat plenty of butter in a frying pan and drop in tablespoons of batter, well apart as they will spread. Fry until golden brown on both sides, turning only once. Serve straight from the pan. Makes about 12 fritters.

Broad Bean and Egg Cheese

*An easily prepared high tea or supper dish for which fresh or frozen beans
are equally suitable.*

1 lb shelled broad beans	**1½ oz flour**
2-3 hard boiled eggs, sliced	**¾ pint full cream milk**
1½ oz butter	**Salt and cayenne pepper**

TOPPING
½ oz butter   **10 oz fresh breadcrumbs**   **2 oz Cheddar cheese, grated**

Set oven to 425°F or Mark 7. Cook the beans in salted water until just soft, then
drain. Meanwhile, hard boil the eggs, allow to cool and then slice. Layer the beans
and egg slices in the bottom of an overproof dish, sandwiching the eggs between
the beans. Melt the butter in a pan, stir in the flour, season, remove from the heat
and stir in the milk. Reheat, stirring, to make a white sauce and pour over the
beans. For the topping, melt the butter in a pan and stir in the breadcrumbs and
cheese until well mixed. Crumble over the sauce and bake for 15 minutes or until
crisp and brown. Serves 4 to 6.

The Old Malt House, Brook, Surrey

Asparagus With Scrambled Eggs

Served on toast this makes a delicate first course or a light supper dish.

12 asparagus spears, cooked and sliced
6 eggs
2 tablespoons double cream

Salt and black pepper
1 oz butter
2 tablespoons Parmesan cheese, grated

Boil the asparagus in the usual way until just tender, then drain and slice. In a bowl, beat the eggs and cream together with a fork until just mixed and season to taste. Melt the butter in pan, add the sliced asparagus and cook gently, stirring, for 1 minute. Pour in the egg mixture and cook over the lowest possible heat, stirring constantly, until the egg begins to set. Stir in the cheese and immediately the egg has set to the preferred consistency, remove from the heat and serve on hot, buttered toast. Serves 2 to 3.

Rhubarb Mould

This simply made sweet is deliciously refreshing on a hot, summer day.

1 lb rhubarb	**Juice of 1 large orange**
6 oz sugar	**4 tablespoons cornflour**

Cut the rhubarb into chunks and put into an enamelled or stainless steel pan. Add the sugar, together with the orange juice made up to $1/2$ pint with cold water. Cover tightly and cook over a low heat for 10 minutes or until the rhubarb has disintegrated. Mash the rhubarb with a wooden spoon and well mix all together. Blend the cornflour to a smooth paste with 6 tablespoons of cold water and stir in to the rhubarb purée. Bring to the boil and cook over a low heat, stirring constantly, for 4 minutes until the mixture has thickened and has lost its floury opaqueness. Pour into a decorative mould rinsed with cold water and put in to the refrigerator to set. Turn out when required and serve cold with single or double cream. Serves 4.

Potato Barley Soup

A thick and satisfying soup which also makes a main course for a light supper,
served with crusty bread.

1 oz butter
1 large onion, peeled and finely chopped
$^1/_4$ lb button mushrooms, sliced
$^1/_4$ lb pearl barley, soaked overnight
   in cold water

2 carrots, scraped and diced
$2^1/_2$ pints beef stock
2 large potatoes, peeled and diced
$^1/_2$ pint full cream milk
Salt and pepper

Finely chopped fresh parsley to garnish

Melt the butter in a large saucepan and gently fry the onion, adding the mushrooms, until the onion is golden but not brown. Drain the barley in a sieve and add to the pan with the carrots. Add the stock, stir and bring to the boil. Reduce the heat and simmer for about 20 minutes until the barley and carrots have softened. Add the potatoes and continue cooking for about 15 minutes longer until the potatoes are soft but not mushy. Stir in the milk. The soup should be fairly thick. Season, bring back to the boil, sprinkle over the parsley and serve. Serves 6.

Deep-fried Courgettes

Crisp, batter-coated slices of courgette which particularly make an excellent accompaniment to lamb dishes.

$1/4$ **lb flour**	$1^1/2$ **lb courgettes, trimmed**
$1/4$ **teaspoon salt**	**and sliced thickly**
1 tablespoon olive oil	**Oil for frying**
$1/4$ **pint lukewarm water**	**1 egg white**

Sift the flour and salt into a bowl, make a well in the centre and add the oil and a little of the water. Stir the liquid with a wooden spoon, gradually incorporating the flour, then add the remaining water a little at a time. The batter should be smooth and thick enough to coat the back of the spoon. Cover and set aside for 30 minutes. Meanwhile, trim the courgettes and slice thickly. Heat the oil in a deep-fry pan until very hot. Just before frying, whip the egg white until stiff and fold in to the batter. Put the courgette slices in the batter, lift out with a skewer and drop gently into the hot oil. Turn once. When the slices are golden brown remove from the oil with a slotted spoon and drain on kitchen paper. Keep hot in a serving dish in the oven until all the courgettes are fried and then serve hot. Serves 4 to 6.

Nutty Baked Cabbage

This dish can be served as an accompaniment to meat, or on its own as a light supper dish.

1 small white cabbage, trimmed
   and roughly chopped
1 oz butter
1 oz flour

$^1/_2$ pint milk
4 oz Cheddar cheese, grated
4 oz chopped mixed nuts
Salt and pepper

Set oven to 425°F or Mark 7. Put the cabbage into a pan of boiling, salted water and cook for 3 to 4 minutes until only just tender. Melt the butter in a saucepan, stir in the flour and cook for 3 to 4 minutes. Remove from the heat and stir in the milk. Return to the heat and, stirring, bring to the boil until the sauce thickens; simmer for 5 minutes. Add the cheese and season well. Butter a shallow 2 pint ovenproof dish and arrange layers of the cabbage, sauce and nuts, finishing with a layer of sauce covered with a sprinkling of nuts. Bake for 20 minutes until the top is golden and bubbling. Serves 4.

Onion and Apple Pie

This savoury pie can be served hot or cold. If cold, add 2 to 3 oz grated Cheddar cheese to the onion.

8 oz prepared shortcrust pastry
2 onions, peeled and sliced
A little oil or butter
1 lb cooking apples, peeled, cored and sliced
Salt and black pepper
$\frac{1}{2}$ teaspoon chopped fresh sage
2 teaspoons chopped fresh parsley
1 to 2 tablespoons thick double cream
A little beaten egg to glaze

Set oven to 400°F or Mark 6. Roll out the pastry on a lightly floured surface. Divide in half and use half to line a lightly greased 7 inch flan dish. Sauté the onions in the oil or butter until soft, but still transparent, then drain well. Place half the apple slices on the pastry and top with the onion. Season well, then sprinkle over the herbs. Add the remaining apple slices, then drizzle over the cream. Top with the remaining pastry, sealing the edges well and trimming neatly. Make a steam hole in the centre of the pie and decorate with leaves cut from any pastry trimmings. Brush with beaten egg to glaze and bake for 30 to 40 minutes until the apples are cooked and the pastry golden brown. Serves 4 to 6.

Springtime - an old cottage garden

Cream of Broccoli Soup

A good way to use up a glut of broccoli from the garden.

1 oz butter
1 leek, thinly sliced
1 celery stalk, thinly sliced
1 lb broccoli heads, broken into
 individual florets

1 small potato, thickly sliced
1½ pints chicken stock
¼ pint single cream
Salt and black pepper
Lemon juice

Small croûtons to garnish

Melt the butter in a large pan, add the leek and celery, cover and cook until they are soft but not browned. Add the broccoli florets, the potato slices and the stock to the pan, cover and simmer gently until all the vegetables are soft. When soft, purée in a food processor or blender, return to the pan and add the cream. Season to taste and add a few drops of lemon juice to intensify the flavour. Re-heat, bringing back just to boiling point but do not let it boil. Serve hot, garnished with croûtons. Serves 4 to 6.

Potato Pancakes

These thin pancakes make an accompaniment for meat or are delicious eaten with a sprinkling of sugar or spread with jam or apple sauce topped with plain yoghurt.

3 lb floury potatoes, peeled	**2 tablespoons flour**
1 small onion, peeled	**Salt**
2 eggs, lightly beaten	**Oil for frying**

Peel the potatoes and grate them into a colander lined with a double thickness of muslin, set over a large bowl. Draw up the muslin and squeeze out as much moisture as possible into the bowl. Let the liquid stand until the starch has settled to the bottom, then carefully pour off the liquid into a jug and reserve. Mix the grated potatoes into the starch, grate in the onion, add the beaten eggs, flour and salt to taste and beat well with a wooden spoon until blended. The mixture should have a dropping consistency; if necessary beat in some of the reserved potato water. Heat the oil in a large frying pan and, when very hot, drop in heaped spoonfuls of batter and spread out thinly. When brown, turn over and brown on the other side. These pancakes are best served straight from the pan, but can be kept hot, singly or in pairs on a baking sheet in a warm oven. Makes about 12 pancakes.

Mustard Glazed Turnips

A first rate accompaniment to lamb, pork or ham and to vegetable pies, flans and cutlets. Always use Dijon, never English, mustard.

2 oz butter
2 lb small, young turnips, peeled
¼ pint chicken stock

1 teaspoon Demerara sugar
Salt and black pepper
2 teaspoons Dijon mustard

2 tablespoons finely chopped parsley

Melt the butter in a large, heavy pan until frothy. Add the turnips, turn to coat with butter and cook over a moderate heat for about 10 minutes, shaking frequently so the turnips fry to a deep golden colour. Reduce the heat, pour in the stock, add the sugar and season to taste. Bring to simmering point, cover and cook for about 20 minutes, shaking occasionally, until the turnips are tender. Transfer with a slotted spoon to a large plate. Stir the mustard into the pan juices, check the seasoning, return the turnips to the pan and re-heat, swirling them around to coat them with the glaze. Transfer to a warmed serving dish and sprinkle with parsley to serve. Serves 6.

Spinach Casserole

Fresh or frozen spinach can be used for this supper dish.

2 lb spinach, cooked and drained
   or frozen spinach, thawed
Salt and pepper
Juice of ½ lemon
4 oz cooked ham or gammon, chopped

1 oz butter
6 oz button mushrooms
2 eggs
4 oz Cheddar cheese, grated
2 tablespoons single cream

Set oven to 400°F or Mark 6. If using fresh spinach, wash well, put into a saucepan, cover and simmer for a few minutes in its own moisture. Drain well. Chop the spinach, season and sprinkle over the lemon juice. Mix in the chopped cooked ham or gammon and put into a greased ovenproof dish. Melt the butter in a pan, cook the mushrooms and arrange them on top of the spinach mixture. Beat the eggs in a bowl, season, add the cheese and cream, mix well and then pour over the mushrooms. Bake for 25 minutes and serve. Serves 4.

Curried Stuffed Marrow

This is a spicy variation to a very traditional English dish.

3 medium onions, peeled and diced
1 tablespoon oil
1 tablespoon curry powder
2 tablespoons flour
2 eating apples, peeled, cored
    and diced

1 pint chicken stock
2 tablespoons chutney
Salt and pepper
1 lb cooked lamb, minced
1 medium size marrow,
    halved and de-seeded

Set oven to 350°F or Mark 4. In a large saucepan, fry the onions in the oil until golden brown. Stir in the curry powder and cook for 2 minutes. Stir in the flour and cook for a further 2 minutes. Add the apples and gradually stir in the stock. Mix well, bring to the boil and simmer for a few minutes. Add the chutney, season, cover and simmer for 30 minutes. Then stir in the minced lamb. Put the mixture into the marrow halves, bring them together carefully and wrap in kitchen foil. Place in a baking tin and bake for $^3/_4$ to 1 hour until the marrow is tender, but do not overcook. Serve sliced. Serves 4 to 6.

Onion and Bacon Roly Poly

A crisp, suet crust encloses a tasty bacon, cheese and onion filling.

1/2 lb self-raising flour	4 rashers bacon, de-rinded and
1 teaspoon baking powder	roughly chopped
1/2 teaspoon salt	1 tablespoon oil
4 oz prepared suet	6 oz strong Cheddar cheese, grated
Water to mix	1 teaspoon chopped fresh sage
3 medium onions, peeled and sliced	1 beaten egg to seal

Set oven to 375°F or Mark 5. Sift the flour, baking powder and salt into a mixing bowl, stir in the suet and add sufficient cold water to make a fairly stiff dough. Roll out on a floured surface to a rectangle about 12 inches x 6 inches. Fry the onions and bacon in the oil until just cooked. Allow to cool and spread over the pastry. Sprinkle over the grated cheese and top with the sage. Brush the edges of the pastry with beaten egg, roll up like a Swiss Roll and seal the ends. Put on a lightly greased baking sheet, make diagonal cuts across the top and bake for about 1 hour until golden brown and crisp. Serves 4.

A cottage at Witley, Surrey

Rhubarb Chutney

This is an excellent way to use up the glut of rhubarb which most home gardeners experience.

4 lb rhubarb, trimmed and cut into small pieces	**1 lb raisins**
	2 level teaspoons ground ginger
1 lb onions, skinned and diced	**2 level teaspoons curry powder**
2 lb Demerara sugar	**1½ pints malt vinegar**

Place the rhubarb, onions, sugar, raisins, spices and 1/2 pint of the vinegar in a large, thick-based saucepan and cook gently until the rhubarb is soft and tender. Add the rest of the vinegar and continue cooking steadily, stirring occasionally until a thick consistency is reached. Put into clean warm jars and cover.

Brussels Sprouts in Cream

Although a little more trouble to make than plain boiled, sprouts served in this way more than repay the effort involved.

1 lb Brussels sprouts	**1 oz butter**
Salt and black pepper	**1 tablespoon flour**
2 oz lean ham, finely diced	**8 tablespoons double cream**

1 oz Gruyàre cheese, grated

Set oven to 375°F or Mark 5. Prepare the sprouts and boil in salted water for 5 minutes. Drain and then toss them in the pan over a low heat to dry them. Remove the sprouts from the heat, add the diced ham and toss together. Melt the butter in an ovenproof dish large enough to hold the sprouts in a single layer. Put the sprouts and ham into the dish, spread out and season to taste. Cover and bake for 10 minutes. In a bowl, blend the flour smoothly with the cream. Remove the sprouts from the oven, fold in the cream mixture and sprinkle over the grated cheese. Return to the oven and continue baking, un-covered, for 15 to 20 minutes until the sauce is bubbling and golden brown on top. Serve straightaway. Serves 4-6.

Lettuce Soufflé

Surplus lettuces can be used to make this unusual accompaniment to roast lamb. It also makes a light supper dish served with poached eggs.

2 large cabbage lettuces	1 lb cooked mashed potato
1 oz butter	2 eggs, separated
2 tablespoons flour	Salt and black pepper
3 spring onions, finely chopped	Lemon juice
2 oz ham, diced (optional)	2 tablespoons Parmesan cheese, grated

Set oven to 375°F or Mark 5. Wash the lettuces, keeping whole, and shake dry. Put into a heavy saucepan, cover and cook over a high heat for 5 minutes. Drain, press out as much water as possible then chop very finely or purée in a food processor or blender. Melt the butter in a pan, blend in the flour and cook over a low heat, stirring constantly, for 2 to 3 minutes. Mix in the lettuce purée, the onions and ham (if used) and cook, stirring for a further 1 minute. Remove from the heat, beat in the mashed potato, the egg yolks, seasoning and a few drops of lemon juice. Whisk the egg whites until stiff and fold gently into the mixture with a metal spoon. Spoon into a soufflé dish, sprinkle with grated cheese and bake for 30 minutes or until puffed up and golden. Serve immediately. Serves 4.

Baked Asparagus

This is a useful and economical way of making a little asparagus go a long way;
it is a good accompaniment to all white meat dishes. The addition of some
diced ham turns it into a main meal.

¹/₂ **lb macaroni**	¹/₂ **pint single cream**
Salt and black pepper	**2 eggs, beaten**
¹/₂ **lb asparagus**	**5 tablespoons Parmesan cheese, grated**
	1 tablespoon butter

Set oven to 400°F or Mark 6. Boil the macaroni in a pan of salted water, following the instructions on the packet. Meanwhile, cut the asparagus into ³/₄ inch lengths and parboil in salted water, just enough to cover, until half cooked - about 6 minutes. Drain the asparagus over the pan of boiling macaroni. Heat the cream in a pan and, when hot, drop in the asparagus and simmer for 2 minutes. Season and set aside. Drain the macaroni, return to the dry pan and stir with a wooden spoon over a low heat for a minute or two to dry off. Then mix in the asparagus/cream, the 2 beaten eggs and 3 tablespoons of the cheese. Pour into a well buttered ovenproof dish, sprinkle with the remaining cheese and dot with butter. Bake for 20 to 25 minutes until set and the top is golden and bubbling. Serve hot. Serves 4.

Jerusalem Artichoke Soup

A delicately flavoured soup - ideal for a dinner party.

1 lb Jerusalem artichokes	**Salt and white pepper**
1 oz butter	**$\frac{1}{2}$ oz cornflour**
1 onion, peeled and chopped	**$\frac{1}{4}$ pint milk**
1 pint chicken stock	**$\frac{1}{4}$ pint single cream**

Fried croûtons for garnish

Prepare the artichokes by peeling as thinly as possible, cut into pieces and drop at once into cold water with a little lemon juice or vinegar added to preserve the colour. Melt the butter in a large saucepan and toss the artichoke pieces and the chopped onion to absorb the fat, but do not allow to colour. Add the stock, season, bring to the boil and simmer for about 45 minutes until the vegetables are tender. Purée in a food processor or blender and return to the rinsed pan. Mix the cornflour with the milk and add to the pan. Bring to the boil, simmer and stir for 3 minutes to thicken. Remove from the heat, allow to cool just a little, then stir in the cream. Reheat if necessary but do not boil. Serve with fried croûtons. Serves 4 to 6.

Parsnip and Cheese Roast

This dish makes a substantial main course served with a green salad. The bacon can be omitted if desired.

2 lb parsnips   2 oz butter   4 rashers smoked streaky bacon, chopped
1 medium onion, peeled and chopped   4 oz Cheddar cheese, grated
8 tablespoons double cream   Salt and black pepper

TOPPING
6 rashers smoked streaky bacon, halved   2 oz Cheddar cheese, grated
4 tablespoons porridge oats

Set oven to 425°F or Mark 7. Scrub the parsnips and boil, whole, in salted water for 15 minutes or until tender. Meanwhile fry the bacon and onion in the butter until the onion is soft and transparent, then set aside. Drain the parsnips, rinse in cold water, trim, rub off the skin with the fingers and chop. Add the chopped parsnips to the onion/bacon mixture in the pan and mash with a fork to a purée. Beat in the cheese and cream and season to taste. Transfer the mixture to a buttered ovenproof dish and pat smooth. Arrange the bacon pieces around the edges of the dish, mix together the cheese and porridge oats and sprinkle thickly over the top. Bake for 20 to 25 minutes or until the topping is golden and bubbling. Serves 4 to 6.

Baked Cheesey Celery

An appetising way of serving cooked celery and, with the addition of extra bacon or chopped ham, it becomes a supper dish.

1 large head of celery, about 2 lbs
1 tablespoon olive oil
6 slices streaky bacon, de-rinded
   and chopped
1 Spanish onion, finely chopped

2 cloves of garlic, crushed
4 medium tomatoes, peeled and chopped
4 tablespoons stock or water
Salt and black pepper
3 oz Parmesan cheese, grated

Set oven to 375°F or Mark 5. Divide the celery stalks, trim and cut into 1 inch pieces. Slit in two if very thick. Fry the bacon in the olive oil until the fat runs, add the onion and garlic and cook, stirring, until soft and golden. Mix in the celery, chopped tomatoes and the stock or water. Season to taste. Cover and cook gently for 20 minutes, stirring occasionally. Using a slotted spoon, transfer the celery, bacon and onion solids to an overproof dish. Reduce the remaining liquid by fast boiling until it thickens somewhat then spoon over the celery. Sprinkle the cheese evenly over the top and bake for about 30 minutes until tender and the top is bubbling and golden brown. Serves 4 to 6.

Spinach Cutlets

Spinach cutlets make a satisfying meal when served with boiled potatoes and a green salad.

1 oz butter
1 medium onion, peeled and chopped
2 lb spinach, cooked and drained
   or frozen spinach, thawed

1 large egg, beaten
4 oz fine dry breadcrumbs
Salt and black pepper
Grated nutmeg

Oil for frying

If using fresh spinach, wash well, put into a saucepan, cover and simmer for a few minutes in its own moisture. Drain well. Chop the spinach. Melt the butter in a pan, add the onion and cook gently until soft and lightly coloured. Remove the pan from the heat, add the spinach, egg and 2 oz of the breadcrumbs. Mix together with a wooden spoon until smoothly blended. Season with salt, pepper and nutmeg. Shape the mixture into 8 flat, oval cakes and coat with dry breadcrumbs. Heat the oil in a large frying pan and fry the cakes on both sides until the crumbs are golden brown and the cutlets are heated right through. Serves 4.

Cabbage and Sausage Casserole

A useful, tasty and inexpensive dish for the winter months.

3 rashers streaky bacon, de-rinded
   and chopped
1 medium onion, peeled and chopped
½ large cooking apple, peeled, cored
   and chopped

1-1¼ lb Savoy cabbage, shredded
Salt and pepper
1 lb pork sausages
Cooking oil
Small potatoes and parsley butter to garnish

Set oven to 400°F or Mark 6. Fry the bacon in a little oil until the fat begins to flow, then add and fry the onion and then the apple, until softened. Wash and drain the shredded cabbage, add to the frying pan, season and cook for about 5 minutes. Transfer all the mixture to an overproof baking dish. Next fry the sausages in a little more oil for about 3 minutes, so as to start the cooking process, then place them on top of the cabbage mixture. Bake in the oven until the sausages are cooked through. Meanwhile, peel and cook sufficient small potatoes as required and boil until tender. Drain, toss in parsley butter, arrange around the sausages and serve. Serves 4 to 6.

Vegetarian Paté

A colourful vegetable and nut paté with an interesting orange flavour.

3 small carrots, scraped and grated

1 small onion, peeled and grated

1 small green pepper, de-seeded and chopped

2 oz small mushrooms, chopped

2 oz chopped mixed nuts

1 small stalk celery with leaves, chopped

1 very small turnip, peeled and grated

Grated rind of 1 small orange

Salt and pepper

1 teaspoon Worcestershire sauce

Good pinch cayenne pepper

$^1/_2$ oz powdered gelatine

3 tablespoons orange juice

Mix together in a bowl all the vegetables, the nuts and the orange rind. Season with salt and pepper to taste and add the Worcestershire sauce and cayenne pepper. Dissolve the gelatine in the orange juice and mix in well. Press the mixture either into a lightly oiled 1 lb loaf tin or into 4 lightly oiled individual soufflé dishes and chill to set. Turn out when required and serve with hot buttered toast. Serves 4.

The Worcestershire Sauce in this recipe will contain a fish product.

Potato Pie

This simple supper dish is often served with pickled beetroot or pickled red cabbage or with crusty brown bread.

2 lb potatoes, peeled and cut into quarters	4 oz strong Cheddar cheese, grated
¼ pint milk	Salt and white pepper
1 oz butter	2 to 3 oz white breadcrumbs, lightly crisped
	A little melted butter for topping

Boil the potatoes in salted water until cooked. Set oven to 425°F or Mark 6. Drain the potatoes well, add the milk and butter and mash until smooth, then stir in the cheese and seasoning. Well butter a 1½ to 2 pint pie dish and sprinkle with the breadcrumbs, pressing them to the base and sides with the back of a spoon. Spoon in the potato and cheese mixture and rough up the top with a fork. Brush with melted butter and bake for 20 to 30 minutes or until golden brown. Serves 4 to 6.

METRIC CONVERSIONS

The weights, measures and oven temperatures used in the preceding recipes can be easily converted to their metric equivalents. The conversions listed below are only approximate, having been rounded up or down as may be appropriate.

Weights

Avoirdupois	Metric
1 oz.	just under 30 grams
4 oz. (¼ lb.)	app. 115 grams
8 oz. (½ lb.)	app. 230 grams
1 lb.	454 grams

Liquid Measures

Imperial	Metric
1 tablespoon (liquid only)	20 millilitres
1 fl. oz.	app. 30 millilitres
1 gill (¼ pt.)	app. 145 millilitres
½ pt.	app. 285 millilitres
1 pt.	app. 570 millilitres
1 qt.	app. 1.140 litres

Oven Temperatures

	°Fahrenheit	Gas Mark	°Celsius
Slow	300	2	150
	325	3	170
Moderate	350	4	180
	375	5	190
	400	6	200
Hot	425	7	220
	450	8	230
	475	9	240

Flour as specified in these recipes refers to plain flour unless otherwise described.